The Earth beneath us

The inside of our planet is constantly on the move, slowly stretching and straining, changing all the time. Rocks have been made and destroyed every minute since the formation of the Earth, 4,600 million years ago.

What is the Earth made of?

At the heart of the movement, 6,380 kilometres below our feet, is the centre or *core* of the Earth. This is made of extremely hot iron and nickel under great pressure.

Temperatures cool down nearer the Earth's surface. The outer skin, or *crust*, is solid. It floats on the softer material beneath it called the *mantle*. The crust itself is like a giant eggshell that has been cracked in places, each section being known as a *plate*. The continents and the seabeds rest on top of these plates.

How rocks are formed

The crust below the continents is about 35-40 kilometres thick, but below the oceans it only averages six kilometres. Liquid rock, or *magma*, can be forced up by the pressure through long and deep cracks in the ocean floor. Here it cools to form solid *igneous* rocks.

The same pressure that pushes these rocks to the surface also pushes against the plates. At the point where one plate meets another, several things can happen. One edge may be pushed up in the air to form a mountain chain. The two edges of the plates may rub against each other, causing earthquakes. Sometimes one plate slips below the other, and melts under the greater temperature. These melted rocks are often forced back to the surface, where they may form solid 'veins' in the existing rock or else break through in the form of a violent volcano.

On the surface of the Earth, wind, water and frost wear down, or *erode*, the rock. Washed or blown away, tiny grains form *sedimentary* rocks such as sandstone.

The changing face of the Earth

Finally, any of these rocks may be squeezed or buried by other rocks or sediment. Under the pressure they are changed into *metamorphic* rocks such as slate.

Mankind has learned to make use of many rocks. By mining we remove these *minerals* from the ground.

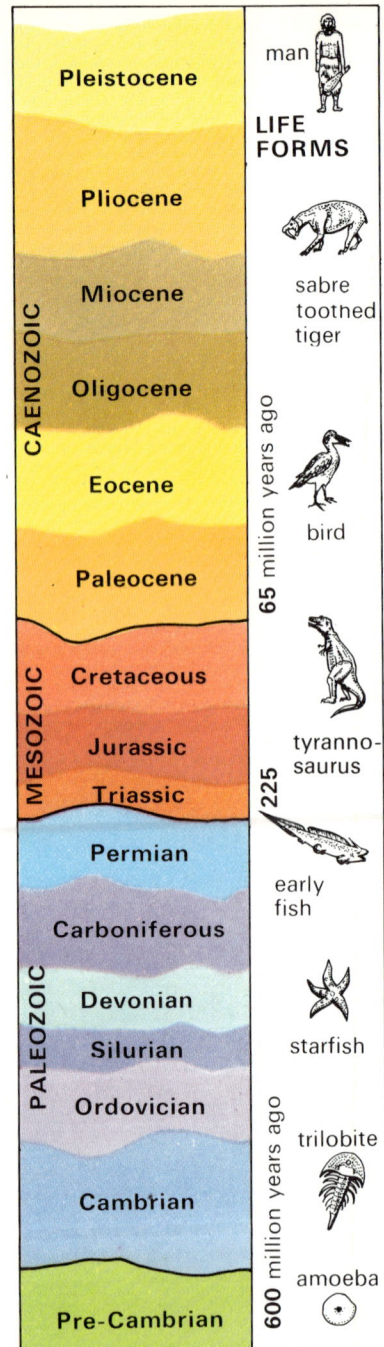

The story of the rocks, showing the main divisions of geological time. The oldest rocks are at the bottom, the youngest at the top.

CAENOZOIC		LIFE FORMS
	Pleistocene	man
	Pliocene	
	Miocene	sabre toothed tiger
	Oligocene	
	Eocene	bird
	Paleocene	65 million years ago
MESOZOIC	Cretaceous	tyrannosaurus
	Jurassic	
	Triassic	225
PALEOZOIC	Permian	early fish
	Carboniferous	
	Devonian	starfish
	Silurian	
	Ordovician	trilobite
	Cambrian	600 million years ago
	Pre-Cambrian	amoeba

INSIDE THE EARTH

Crust
Earth's surface, made up of plates of rock that support the continents and seabeds

Transition layer
Molten and semi-solid rock, thicker than the crust

Upper mantle
Rock under great pressure and heat

Transition layer
400-800 km deep

Lower mantle
Rock under even greater pressure

Outer core
Liquid rock, probably molten iron and nickel

Inner core
Solid iron, nickel and cobalt under tremendous pressure

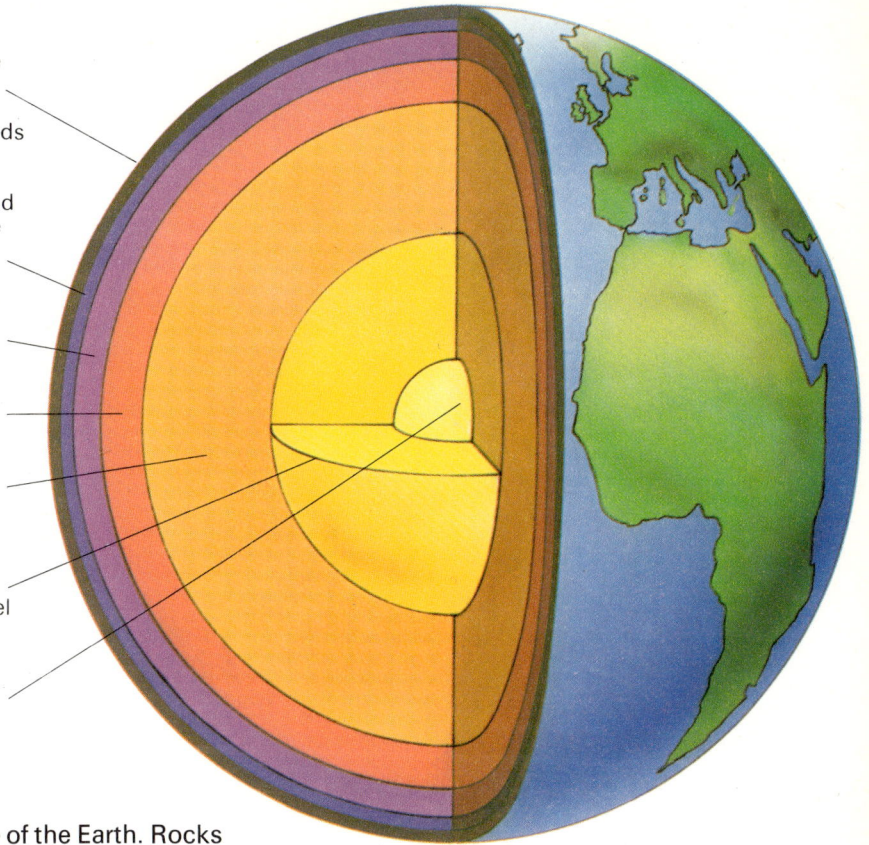

Below: the surface of the Earth. Rocks are crumpled into folds and eroded. Magma is forced up through volcanoes. Man has learned to make use of these mineral resources.

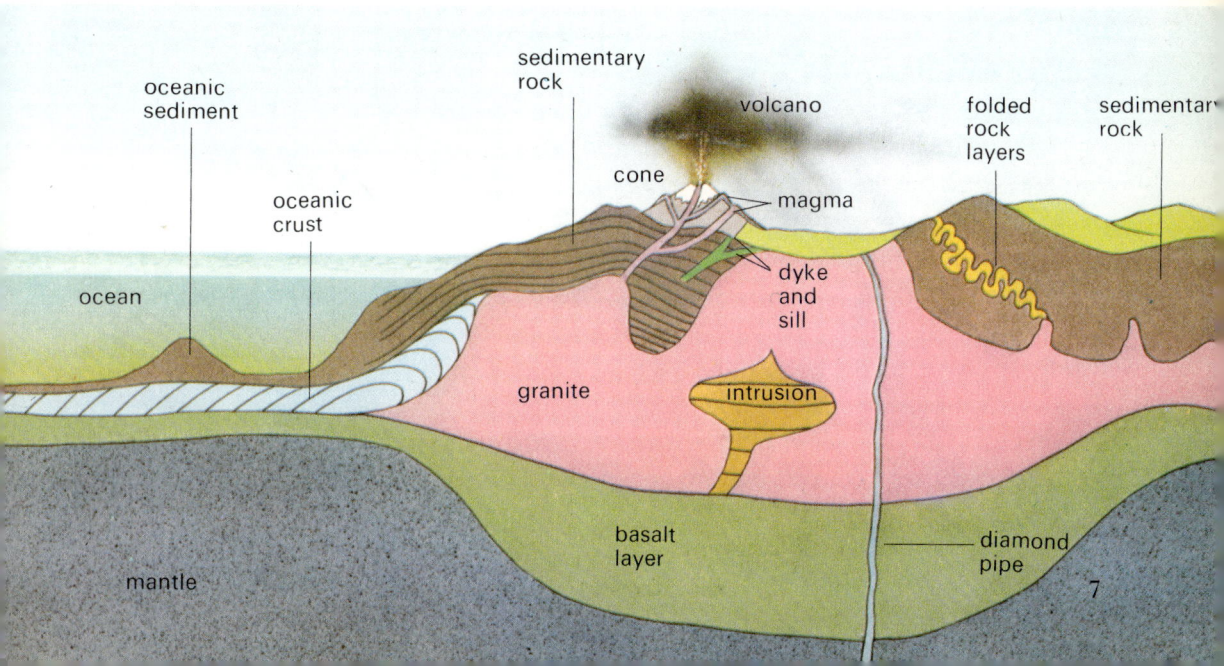

sedimentary rock

oceanic sediment

volcano

folded rock layers

sedimentary rock

oceanic crust

cone

magma

ocean

dyke and sill

granite

intrusion

mantle

basalt layer

diamond pipe

7

The search begins

Man has been a miner for much of his history. Prehistoric man could only survive by learning to use tools and weapons. From picking up sticks and stones he found lying around, man slowly learned to improve them for special purposes. People of this *Stone Age* learned to chip and flake flints until they were razor sharp. Eventually they learned to dig shafts down into chalk to mine the flint.

The use of metals

About 10,000 years ago people around the Mediterranean Sea and in the Middle East began to use metals as well as wood and stone. Copper and gold found on the surface were first used for tools, weapons and ornaments.

About 3500 BC it was discovered that copper became stronger when heated. A little later it was found that bronze—a mixture of copper, zinc and tin—was stronger still. From the Mediterranean region use of these metals gradually spread through Europe. We call these periods the *Copper* and *Bronze Ages*.

About 1200 BC the use of iron weapons and tools, valued for their hardness, became common. At first surface iron was used, but then many underground iron deposits were discovered in the eastern Mediterranean area. *Iron Age* men started to dig down for new sources of metals and search for new mines. Those warriors with the better weapons soon conquered their neighbours.

Old World and New World

Metal became so important that it was used for trade in the form of coins, normally made of gold and silver. Mineral wealth helped to make empires powerful, and many wars were fought over minerals. The Romans, as the Greeks and Egyptians before them, used armies of slaves to work in their mines.

With the discovery of the New World in 1492, European adventurers were lured across the Atlantic by tales of fabulous wealth. Spanish explorers opened up the silver and gold mines of South America. A fortune in gold and silver was shipped back to enrich the countries of Europe.

In the late Stone Age, people learned that by digging underground they could reach the best flints. Rough shafts were dug and flints loosened with antler picks.

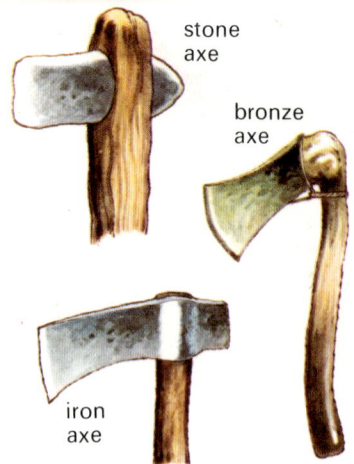

stone axe

bronze axe

iron axe

The first tools and weapons were made of wood and stone. Bronze and then iron were found to be better.

Mines and Mining

Peter Harben

Macdonald Educational

Contents

How to use this book
This book tells you the story of mining, from earliest
times to the present day. The methods of underground
and surface mining are described, and the influence
that the mining industry has on our daily lives. Look
first at the contents page to see if the subject you are
looking for is listed. For instance, if you want to find
out about prospecting, you will see that it is to be
found on page 18. The index will tell you where and
how many times a particular subject is mentioned and
whether there is a picture of it. Dredging, for example,
you will find on pages 32-33. The glossary explains
the more difficult terms found in the book.

Page

Labels on the diagram: sand, boulder clay, flint, soft chalk, hard chalk, shaft, flint

German miners in the sixteenth century. This is a picture from one of the first books on mines and mining, by Georgius Agricola.

Spanish soldiers brought back gold and silver from the newly discovered mines of South America, murdering and enslaving the native Indians.

The Industrial Revolution

The seventeenth century was a period of scientific progress. Many advances were made in mining. In 1627 explosives were used to break rocks for the first time, in what is now Czechoslovakia. In 1698 a British mine was pumped dry by a primitive version of the steam engine. Such new discoveries paved the way for the new age just ahead—the Industrial Revolution.

What was the Industrial Revolution?

Before the 18th century most families in Europe farmed the land and sold their produce at the local market. There were few roads and few large towns. But during the 1700s the population of Europe doubled, and the demand for food and raw materials increased. This demand was met by a series of important inventions which changed society dramatically.

This new machine age, which we call the Industrial Revolution, started in Great Britain. People flooded into the new industrial centres such as London, Liverpool and Manchester to work in factories. The new age depended on natural resources, in particular iron and coal. Mining became the key to the modern world.

Metals and machines

The first industrial machinery was made of wood and powered by water. Then came larger machines made of iron. Although iron had been used for centuries,

Above: mining during the Industrial Revolution was dangerous. Gas explosions were common.

Below: young children were forced to work under terrible conditions in Victorian coal mines.

charcoal was needed to *smelt* the iron (or melt it down in order to purify it). Charcoal is obtained from partly burnt wood and wood was in short supply. In 1735 however Abraham Darby produced *coke* by baking coal in airless ovens to remove gas and tar vapour. Coke could now be used for smelting instead of charcoal.

Britain became the world's leading producer of iron—and also of copper, lead, zinc and tin. With inventions such as the Bessemer process for making steel from cast iron (1856), Britain became a great industrial power.

Industry was now powered by the steam engine, an invention patented by James Watt in 1769. At first mainly used for pumping water from mines, it was soon used for all kinds of machinery including the coal-fired railway engine. By 1840 over 8,000 km of track had been laid in Britain alone. Canals, barges, trains and steamships enabled goods to be transported quickly.

Conditions in the mines

Many fortunes were made at this time—but at a price. The new energy created riches for the mine owners, but poverty for the mine workers and their families. Working and living conditions were grim. Work in the mines was dangerous and many miners were killed in accidents. Men, women and even small children were forced to work long hours underground. Children were employed to haul heavy trucks of coal with chains and to open trap doors in the tunnels. The miners faced a long hard struggle to improve their conditions.

Above: Humphry Davy (1778-1829) invented a Safety Lamp which gave light underground without the danger of igniting gas.

Below: a French coal mine of 1885. The Industrial Revolution spread throughout Europe.

A new age

From the middle of the last century the mines of Europe had competition. The importance of Britain's mines grew less as the vast riches of other continents were discovered. New lands were explored and settled.

Gold rush fever

In many parts of the world deposits of minerals were discovered at a whirlwind pace. It was an exciting age. When news of gold leaked out, thousands of men left home in the hope of making a fortune, and made journeys to distant lands.

Finding a likely spot, the miner would 'stake his claim'—mark out the area with stakes, so claiming a legal right to whatever he found. Often the land really belonged to someone else already and fights would break out over the claim. Then the miner would begin the back-breaking work of 'panning' for gold—washing gravel in search of the tell-tale glitter of gold.

Many a claim proved to be worthless. In the boom towns that grew up over-night miners would fight and drink in the saloons. But the lucky few did make immense fortunes and became very rich men. When the mining opportunities came to an end, many new towns were suddenly deserted, becoming empty 'ghost' towns.

Around the world

The mining boom started in the early 1840s with the discovery of copper in Australia and the USA. In 1849 gold found in California lured thousands of men westwards.

Rich sources were discovered all over

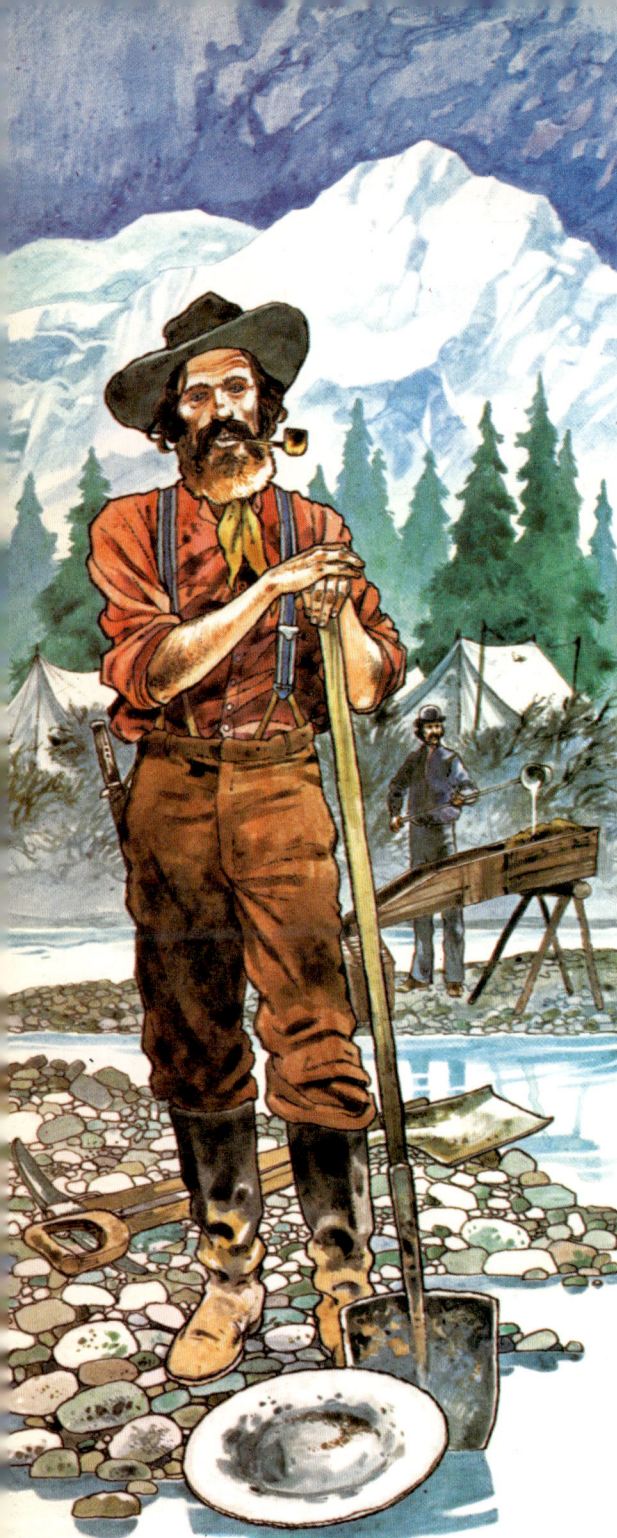

Panning for gold in the Yukon in the 1890s. The miners are washing gravel from the river bed, in the hope of making a fortune.

America. Silver, iron ore, coal and phosphate discoveries added to the wealth of the USA. Asbestos, gold, copper, lead and zinc were found in Canada, where in 1897 the discovery of gold in the Yukon region caused another gold rush. South and Central America became an important source of minerals. Copper and nitrate deposits were found in Chile, tin in Bolivia and oil in Venezuela.

Prospectors also pushed into Africa, Asia and Australia. In Africa enormous deposits of gold, diamonds, copper and platinum were found, and in Australia the rich Broken Hill mine and the gold-fields of Kalgoorlie.

Industrial needs

Fed by these newly discovered resources, large industrial areas had now grown up in many parts of the world. The twentieth century became the age of new machinery, of new factories, cars, ships and aeroplanes. Steel, coal and oil became more and more important, and with them the whole mining industry.

Working conditions

Conditions in the mines of late nineteenth century Europe improved only very slowly. Women and children were no longer employed, but wages were low and accidents, illness and loss of life were still common. Miners in many countries went on strike to improve their working conditions, particularly in the hungry years of the 1920s and 1930s.

As the twentieth century went on, safety in the mines improved, helped by new inventions. Many jobs once done by men were now done by machines. The mining industry became more efficient and the miner himself became a skilled technician in a vital industry.

Above: mining before the First World War. Before the automatic cutting machines of today, all work was done with pick, shovel and crowbar. This back-breaking work was carried out in very cramped conditions.

Below: British miners on strike in 1921. Between the wars life was very hard for miners, in both Europe and America.

A miner's life

Times have changed. The modern coal mine looks more like a light engineering works than the old-fashioned mine. Machinery has changed the work of the miner considerably. Giant cutters, loaders and conveyor belts have come to his aid. Mechanical tools have replaced the pick for working smaller seams.

Even so, the job is a tough and demanding one. The miner spends much of his life underground, often in cramped conditions. Dust from coal and other minerals can cause lung disease, and the fear of accidents remains. But modern emphasis on safety and efficiency has improved mining's record.

Mining today

Many mining communities are at the centre of large industrialized areas, where surrounding factories depend on the mine's output for power or raw materials. But many communities are in lonely places far from cities.

This isolation, together with a history of shared hardship and self-sufficiency, has often made the mining town or village a closely knit community. Mining still runs in many families and often sons follow their fathers in learning the skills of the miner.

A special bond can grow up between those who work together underground. This feeling is often reflected in the miner's out-of-work activities. European miners' choirs and brass bands have become famous all over the world.

Coming on shift

What is it like to work at an underground coal mine? Arriving at the mine, our

Above: Durham miners' gala. Bands and miners with trade union banners parade through this northern English town.

Below: a modern mining town. Kiruna, in the north of Sweden, has green trees and new flats around its iron ore mines.

Above: the end of a hard day's work. Miners from the Broken Hill lead/zinc mine in Australia leave the 'cage'.

Below: a Yorkshire miner has a shower to wash off the coal dust. Modern mines have showers and recreation halls.

miner changes into the 'uniform' necessary to work underground—overalls, black leather belt, helmet, steel toe-capped boots, leather pads to protect the knees, and a pair of leather gloves. Then he collects his lamp and battery from the lamproom.

The battery, which is the size of a medium packet of soap powder, only much heavier, is fixed to the leather belt. The lamp clips to the helmet. The miner is now ready to go underground.

Going underground

Before the miner's journey down through the long shaft linking the surface with the mine below, he and his shift are searched for cigarettes and matches—deadly objects when mixed with the explosive gases that sometimes linger in coal mines.

A set of bell signals from the bottom of the shaft to the top tells the hoist operator that all is ready. The 'cage', or lift, carrying the men and the equipment, descends to the depths.

The mine

At the foot of the shaft the area is usually large and light, with maintenance bays and offices. Often a processing plant is to be found underground too. Here the material that has been mined is broken down. As much of the work as possible in the mine is done by machines, although many tasks must still be done by men. Trains carry the miner to the face. Other trains carry coal to be processed.

The end of the shift

At the end of their shift, the men return to the surface in the cage. The lamps are left in the lamproom, where the batteries are recharged for the next day. The men go off to have a shower and wash off the grime, and then go home.

Why do we mine?

Minerals are hard workers for mankind. All the work that goes into mining, and the processing of the mined material, has one aim: to provide mankind with *end-products* that have many uses in everyday life.

Abrasives and gemstones

Since early times beautiful and hard-wearing stones have been in demand for work and wear. Diamonds are so hard that they are of great value to industry for drilling and cutting. The beauty and hardness of many stones have also made them precious ornaments, used to decorate rings, necklaces and brooches. Sand is useful in rubbing a surface smooth: it is an *abrasive*.

Metals and their use

Gold and silver are metals that have long been used for coinage, although they are now so valuable that *alloys*, or mixtures, of cheaper metals are usually used.

Everything from cars to buildings contains iron, which is cheap, strong and plentiful. Metals like zinc are good protection against rust. Indoors, electricity can pass easily through copper and lightweight aluminium—they are excellent 'conductors' of electricity and are therefore used in electrical parts.

Energy, heating and insulation

Combustible materials are those that are easy to burn. Coal, oil (petroleum) and natural gas are examples of minerals that heat our homes and supply power for our industries. Now materials such as uranium are also providing radioactive energy. Some materials resist heat. The most widely used is asbestos.

Household helpers

Combustible material may often be treated and processed to produce valuable *by-products*, such as wax, plastic and nylon. Clays, which are soft and easily shaped when wet, but rigid and strong when heated, make bricks and pottery.

Feeding mankind

Salt is one mineral essential for human life and chemical fertilizers like potassium, phosphorus and nitrogen also feed the crops that eventually feed mankind.

FERTILIZERS
Minerals used for fertilizer include potash, phosphates, borates, nitrates, magnesite.

COINAGE
Coins exchange hands every minute of the day. Metals used include gold, silver, copper, nickel and alloys.

PLASTICS
Plastic and nylon (by-products of coal and oil) are used for packaging, clothing, machinery—and toys.

ABRASIVES
The wall is being sanded down by the builders. Common abrasives are sand and emery.

IRON AND STEEL
Iron, steel, zinc and alloys of iron are widely used for building, machinery, vehicles, tools and household equipment.

GLASS
Minerals used in glass making are sand, limestone, dolomite, soda ash and felspar.

MINING PRODUCTS
Look closely at this everyday street scene. How many items can you see that are end-products of mining? All sorts of objects that we take for granted, have their origins in minerals that must be extracted from the ground.
Minerals have different qualities. Some are valued for their hardness, heaviness or transparency. Others provide energy or conduct electricity.

CONSTRUCTION
Sand, gravel, limestone, clay and slate are just a few of the many materials used in the building industry.

ELECTRICAL PARTS
The builder is reeling out electric cable. Copper, aluminium and gold are used for electric parts.

FUELS
The car runs on petrol. Coal, oil, gas, asphalt, tar sands and radioactive minerals such as uranium are also sources of energy.

Prospecting

The search for mineral wealth is an exciting detective story. The *prospector*, the person who seeks out mineral deposits, must look for clues which will lead him to his goal.

As we have seen, minerals and metals are found both underground and on the surface. Surface mining is known as *opencast* mining. Most surface deposits that are known to be useful are already being mined, and so the worldwide search has gone underground. A geologist must now search through tonnes and tonnes of rocks. The *orebody* (deposit of ore) or *petroleum reservoir* (layer of oil) can be buried as much as 12,000 metres below the ground.

Aerial survey

Surprisingly enough, the modern search for mineral deposits often begins at a great distance *above* the possible site. Photographs from orbiting satellites show areas the size of Italy in one picture and aeroplanes can photograph large cities in one frame.

With such techniques, today's geologist can see the arrangement of rocks in any given area. In remote areas these aerial maps are sometimes the only ones available to the prospector.

Down to earth

An exploration programme is very much like using a zoom lens in a camera—at first the whole area is surveyed and then gradually the field is narrowed down to a close-up.

Other clues should not be overlooked. One method is simply chatting with an old-time local prospector, or looking

Above: the traditional way of finding underground water or metals. The Y-shaped twig is said to twitch in the hands of a good 'dowser' or 'diviner'.

Below: a geologist examines rock in Alaska. The modern prospector uses scientific methods to find mineral deposits.

through records of mining activity in days past.

After a likely area has been pin-pointed, the geologist follows in the prospector's footsteps and takes a look himself. If the area is difficult to reach a helicopter can be used to scout around and collect samples of rock.

The type of rock on the surface can tell an experienced geologist just what minerals and metals to expect down below. Tin, for example, is often found together with granite.

Searching for clues

Fortunately metals and minerals give themselves away. Even at great depths, certain physical qualities such as magnetism and electrical conductivity can be measured at the surface.

Samples of soil, river water and stream sediments are collected and tested for unusually high quantities of chemicals. This can reveal more information about mineral deposits underground.

With all these methods and measurements at his disposal, the geologist can get a good idea which areas provide the best prospects. Some are singled out for closer study. By digging a trench or shallow pit, geologists can examine a shallow orebody at first hand.

If it is necessary to go deeper, a drill continues their search.

Mapping the minerals

If the clues remain promising, a number of other holes are drilled on a regular grid pattern—just like a chess board—to outline the exact shape and size of the suspected ore-body and estimate the amounts of valuable material. If all these clues point to a worthwhile deposit, the mining operation can now begin.

Above: photographs from space showing rock formations on the surface of Earth. This picture shows the mining country of the Kentucky border, USA.

Below: searching for nickel in Western Australia. Drills are mobile and can be put on the back of a truck for use in the bush.

Underground mining

Some miners have to travel over three kilometres to work—downwards. Over the centuries man has tunnelled through and shifted countless tonnes of rock in an effort to mine everything from sandstone to gold. The rich gold mines of South Africa are now extracting ore 4,000 metres below the ground.

Shafts and tunnels

The basic principles of underground mining have changed little over the years, although of course machinery has changed the scale of the operation. A 3,000 year-old underground copper mine recently discovered at Timna, Israel, was found to be 'modern' enough to have a ventilation system.

In most cases the valuable material, or orebody, is reached by a vertical *shaft* from the surface. A number of interconnecting tunnels run into the various parts of the orebody.

Normally a second vertical shaft is cut to provide a through draught of air for ventilation. Most modern mines have strong fans or suction pipes to help the air flow along.

Digging the ore

The ore itself is usually drilled and then blasted to break and loosen it. Holes drilled in a particular pattern are filled with exact amounts of explosive. This is detonated, or set off, and the required amount of ore is freed. The cleared area forms a huge underground room known as a *stope*.

The broken ore is removed from the stope by truck, locomotive or conveyor belt and taken to a skip or cage. It is then raised to the surface by a powerful hoist.

An underground city

Many mines are vast organizations, like great underground cities. They have their own road systems and traffic laws. Engineers and geologists scurry around, often on electric carts, and it is a hive of activity. Safety is a major concern. Inspectors try to ensure that the steel supported tunnels and shafts are large and airy, that the lighting is good and the transport systems safe.

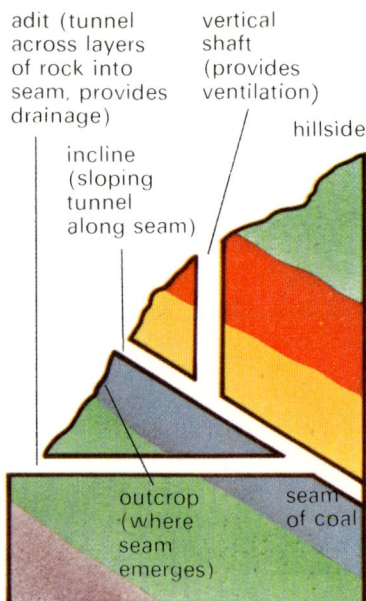

adit (tunnel across layers of rock into seam, provides drainage)

vertical shaft (provides ventilation)

hillside

incline (sloping tunnel along seam)

outcrop (where seam emerges)

seam of coal

Tunnelling into the side of a hill. The adit leads into the seam of coal. A vertical shaft provides ventilation.

The roof of this mine is supported by hydraulic props. Fluid inside the metal props keeps them firm despite pressure and ground movement.

Right: drilling at the face is one of the hardest jobs in an underground mine. Here in the gold mines of South Africa the face may be up to 4,000 metres underground. Temperatures are high and conditions cramped. Water can seep from the rocks and cause flooding.

The bit, or cutting end of the drill, is cooled by water, which also reduces the dust. In some mines machines are used which can drill several holes at the same time.

Below: in modern coal mines giant cutting machines are used. Since coal is relatively soft, they can cut and break coal away from the seam. The coal then falls on to a conveyor belt, which carries it away.

A coal mine

The story of coal, one of man's most useful sources of energy, goes back more than two hundred million years. In the Carboniferous period (*see page 6*) swamps and forests covered large areas. Over many thousands of years dead trees and plants became buried under rock. Under the pressure, they were forced into seams of coal. The best coal is *anthracite*, which is rich in carbon and therefore burns well. More recently formed coal is softer and contains less carbon. It is called *lignite* or brown coal.

A coal mine is an enormous and complicated organization. The twin shafts provide a ventilation system as much as four kilometres underground. The shafts are connected to a network of tunnels leading to the face. Here cutting machines gouge out the coal. Narrow seams are worked by miners with drills.

tips

drilling to place explosives

shuttle car

conveyor belt

coal train

face

loader

cutting machine

pithead

winding gear (encased)

shower rooms, canteen and recreation building

landscaping

railway link

this gap represents the depth of the shaft

shaft two

shaft one

cage

offices

first aid room

air pump

hydraulic props

Oil and natural gas

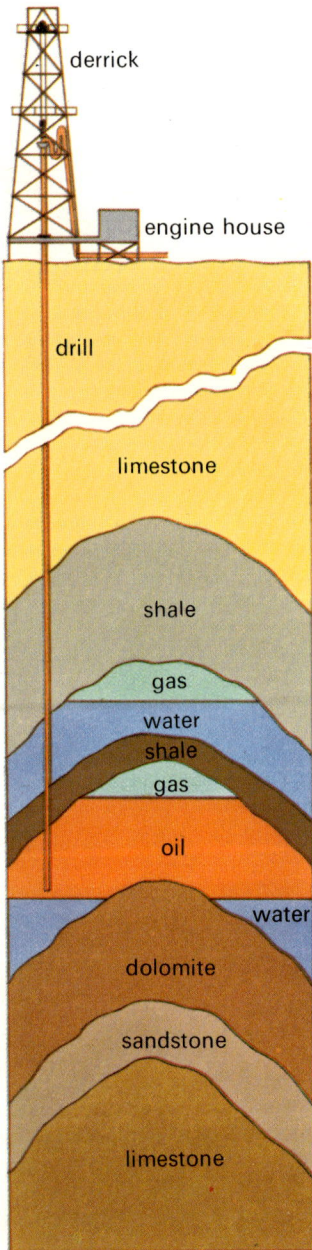

derrick

engine house

drill

limestone

shale

gas

water

shale

gas

oil

water

dolomite

sandstone

limestone

Oil and natural gas are trapped in porous rocks, which are capped by non-porous rocks. When a drill pierces the cap, the fluid is forced up by pressure.

Among the most useful resources to be extracted from the depths of the Earth are oil and natural gas. Their origins go back millions of years and they were formed in much the same way as coal, only out of different kinds of living matter. Plants and minute water animals died and were buried in their millions by the mud of the shallow seas and lakes in which they lived.

Under pressure of the rocks under which they became buried, their remains were eventually changed into the 'hydrocarbons' that oil and natural gas are made of. Porous or absorbent rocks like sandstone soak up these deposits like a giant sponge. When this drenched rock is capped by another rock that is not porous, such as shale, the oil is trapped.

Drilling for oil

In order to extract this oil, surveys of the area are completed and tests are carried out. The drilling *rig* is erected. A *derrick* or framework supports a diamond-headed *bit*, the cutting end which bores down through thousands of metres of rock, connected to the rig by lengths of rigid steel piping. When the cap of rock is pierced, the oil is forced to the surface in a 'gusher'—a great spurt of oil. This is sealed off and piped.

The oil that comes to the surface is a dark, sticky liquid. This petroleum or *crude oil* must go through stages of *refinement* or purification, before it can be used by us. Oil and liquified natural gas are piped and shipped to the refineries. In the USA alone there is enough oil pipeline to go around the world nine times! Convoys of giant sea tankers, some weighing over 250,000 tonnes each, also carry the precious material to distant lands.

The oil industry

Early production came from small amounts of oil which seeped up to the surface. Large scale production began in Romania in 1857, and the American oil boom began with the discovery of oil in Pennsylvania in 1859.

In the early days finding the oil was largely a matter of luck. Men would drill 'wildcat' wells at random in areas they thought promising, hoping to strike it rich.

Up to about 1900, the world's oil production was only 150 million barrels a year. (Oil is usually measured in 'barrels'—35 US gallons). Today's consumption is enormous—around 20,000 million barrels a year. As we use up supplies, a scientific approach is required.

Natural gas, originally burnt off at the well head as waste, is now used as an important source of energy. The search for oil and gas is now based on the study of fossils and geology.

Across the world

Great deposits of oil are now being drilled in the Middle East, Nigeria, USA, Venezuela and the Gulf of Mexico. Conditions can be tough. In Europe the North Sea field is under more than 150 metres of water.

With the ever increasing use of fuel for cars, diesel trains, aircraft, and the great demand for the by-products of oil—soaps, plastic, nylon, chemicals, fertilizers and even perfumes—oil has become more important than any other mineral or metal.

Above: the Alaska pipeline brings oil and gas across Canada to the USA.

Below: obtaining oil from far beneath the waves of the North Sea.

Opencast mining

Opencast, open pit, and surface mining all mean the same thing: digging material from the surface of the Earth instead of tunnelling down to it. It is relatively easy, economical and very common. The earliest type of mining, it has been in use since the Stone Age, when flint was often mined in this way. Today the scale is greater. The equipment and scientific skills used in this open-air mining are also more advanced but the operation is still basically that of removing useful minerals from the Earth's surface.

Mining without a roof

There are three main types of opencast mining. Firstly minerals may be simply scraped from the surface. Secondly a long bed of material may be dug out just below the surface. Finally a deep pit may be cut into the ground to mine a massive buried deposit. Most pits go down in a series of steps or benches, many 15 metres high and sometimes 10 metres wide. As the mine goes deeper, the steps become wider to allow a gradual and stable slope downwards. There is always a danger of landslide into this man-made terraced valley. Underground water too can pose a problem by flooding workings, which then have to be pumped dry.

Mining in bulk

Nevertheless, opencast mining is the simplest way to remove vast quantities of material. Limestone and clay for example, which are low priced per tonne, must be mined in quantity. Giant trucks can simply drive in and fill up.

On the other hand, improved processing techniques can now take small amounts of valuable material from large amounts of poor quality ore. So what may at first seem to be a poor deposit can today be worth mining after all.

The operations of the Jeffrey mine in Canada are an example of this process. The largest asbestos mine in the world, it must take out 35 million tonnes of rock a year to produce only 700,000 tonnes of asbestos—one fiftieth of the total mined material!

Holes are drilled in a precise pattern

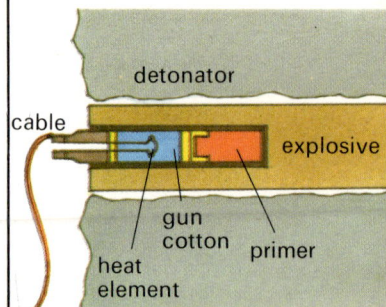

Explosive charges are placed in the holes

The charge is detonated and the rock broken

Above: in both underground mining (top) and surface mining, rock is removed by blasting.
Right: a diamond mine. Opencast mines are often on a vast scale.

Mining monsters

Many opencast mines are so busy that they have a traffic problem. The bottom of the pit is often full of machines digging, cutting, scraping and transporting large tonnages of material. There are a great number of different machines, some of them truly gigantic. One truck can now carry over 200 tonnes in one load—equivalent to 40 elephants!

Most of the vehicles in the pit work in pairs: a digger needs a truck to carry away the load, while the truck often dumps the load on to a conveyor belt.

An army of machines

First the surface soil or *overburden* usually has to be cleared of vegetation by a bulldozer. This may then be coupled to a scraper to give it extra power. This is a long vehicle with a large blade in its belly which digs into the ground to scrape up the loose material.

Next in the plan of attack come the large diggers to bite down into the Earth. These load up the giant trucks, locomotives, or conveyor belts which take the material away for processing.

Other machines like strange, ungainly beasts, continue the work—the dragline for example, a large crane connected to an excavating bucket by a series of wire ropes. There are even 'walking draglines', cranes designed to move on mechanical legs, like some creatures from a science fiction film.

Gouging out the soil

Another interesting machine is the bucket wheel excavator. This consists of a wheel of buckets which rotates and digs into the earth. When the bucket turns upside down, the material falls out and is collected by a conveyor belt. Some of these machines have the ability to dig well over 2,000 tonnes an hour—but at a price: one machine recently cost a mining company $4 million!

Many of the machines used in opencast mining are simply larger versions of the type used in large construction sites and for building motorways. However, the very heavy work and the long hours in use mean that the machines are usually specially made for the job.

Giant draglines can cast out their buckets like a fishing line and 'reel in' the loose material.

Mining trucks may have more than twelve gears and carry enormous loads of 200 tonnes or more.

Gigantic buckets on this wheel excavator bite into loose rock and scoop it up.

An iron ore mine

A modern opencast or surface mine can supply more than 40 million tonnes of rock per year. Often of vast size, their most notable feature is the way that the rock is removed in benches or layers.

This selection of activities at an opencast iron ore mine shows the great array of machinery used to remove the rock. Working together as a team, these machines must be carefully organized Rarely out of work, they often keep production going around the clock to feed the nearby processing plant.

processing plant

railway link

bulldozer

truck

face
shovel

truck

drill

loaders

Mining with water

Water has always created difficulties for the miner, hindering tunnelling and seeping through rock. But there are in fact many mining operations that cannot work without water.

Hydraulic mining

One of the simplest mining methods is *hydraulic* mining. This consists of washing material to the bottom of an opencast mine using high pressure water hoses called *giants* or *monitors*.

The mud or *slurry* is then collected in a trap or sump where it is separated and dried. This approach will only work with soft material like clay, certain tin minerals, or loose overburden.

Dredging

Another kind of mining actually takes place in water. This is dredging, whereby a ship scoops up material from the bottom of a shallow lake, river or sea. With a bucket dredge, a series of large buckets on a revolving belt bite into the material, delivering twenty or thirty bucket loads a minute.

The suction dredge acts like a giant vacuum cleaner. It simply sucks the material up at the rate of about 1,500 tonnes an hour. Dredging is used to gather heavy material like tin, gold, diamonds and titanium—minerals which sink quickly and do not dissolve underwater.

Solution mining

On the other hand, those minerals that do dissolve easily in water are not always lost. Water containing the valuable mineral can be retrieved by *solution mining*. The idea is very simple: a hole is drilled down to, say, a bed of salt or potash. Water is pumped down, the mineral is dissolved and brought to the surface as a solution. The sun or man-made heat dries up the water and leaves the mineral behind.

The Frasch process

The same principle is used in the *Frasch process*, a method of mining sulphur, invented by a German-born American, Herman Frasch (1851–1914). A drill bores down to the deposits of sulphur. The drilling system is

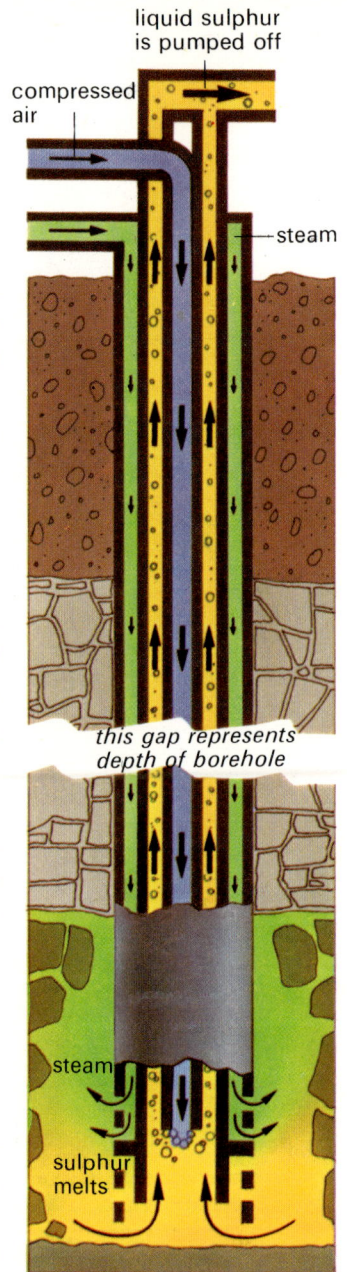

liquid sulphur is pumped off

compressed air

steam

this gap represents depth of borehole

steam

sulphur melts

The Frasch process extracts sulphur from deep underground. Superheated steam melts the sulphur, which is pumped back to the surface through the drilling system.

made up of three pipes, an inner, a middle and an outer. Steam is piped down the outer pipe at great heat, and forced out into the deposits of sulphur, which it melts.

Compressed air is pumped down the inner pipe and this forces the liquid sulphur up the middle pipe. In this way the sulphur is brought to the surface and piped off to be processed.

Sea harvest

The sea and many lakes are natural storehouses containing most minerals and metals including gold. However, at the moment only salt, magnesia and bromine are extracted on a large scale. In many countries the sun can do the hard work by evaporating, or drying out, the water and leaving the mineral to be harvested.

Water has always been essential for man's well-being; for centuries people have dried out sea water under the sun to obtain its salt.

Other vast resources are only now beginning to be fully realised. In the near future nodules of manganese may be mined from deep sea.

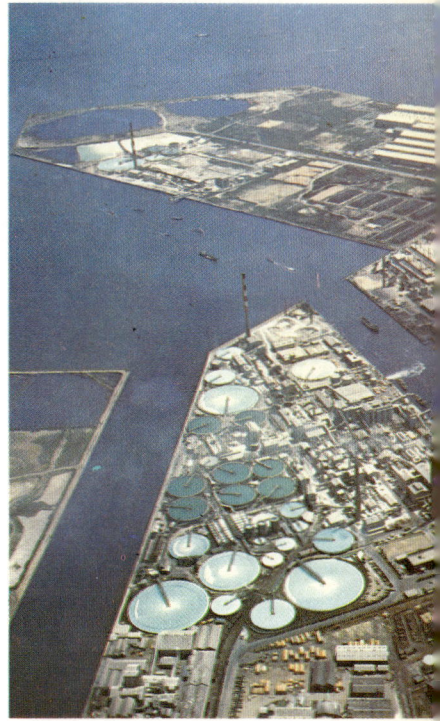

Above: magnesia is extracted from sea water in Japan.

Below: dredges can scoop up minerals from sea or river bed.

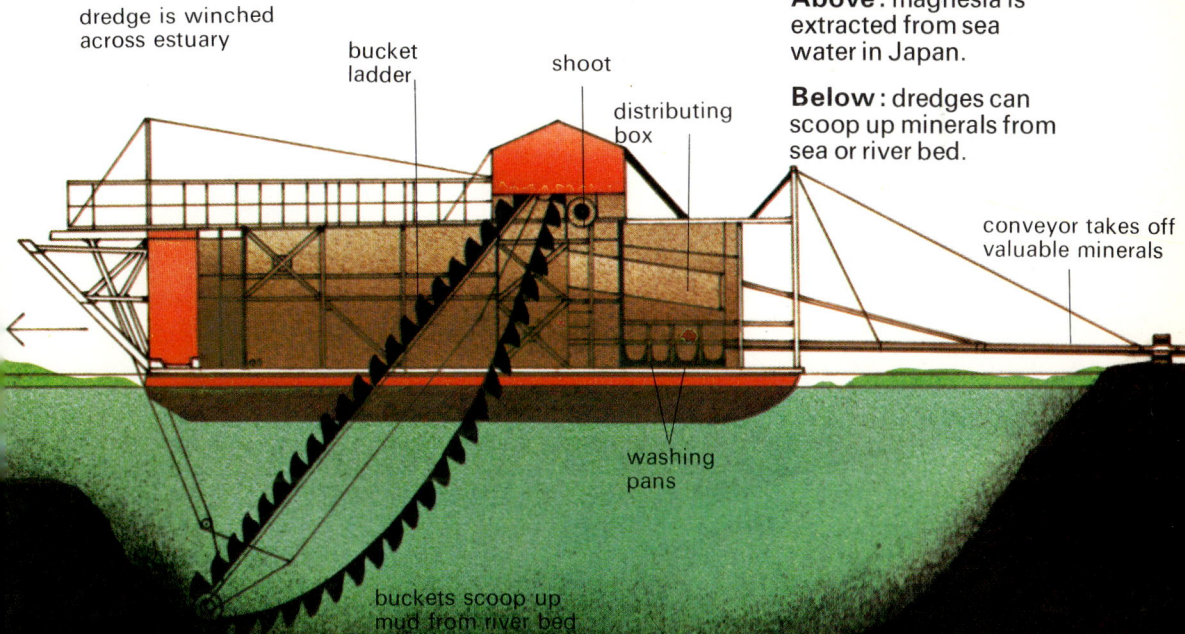

dredge is winched across estuary

bucket ladder

shoot

distributing box

conveyor takes off valuable minerals

washing pans

buckets scoop up mud from river bed

Processing minerals

Few minerals or metals can be used in their natural state since worthless and valuable materials exist together. The mined ore must be processed so that the valuable part of it is extracted and prepared for use.

Breaking down rock

The first step in processing the minerals is breaking the ore down into a manageable size. First a crusher shatters the rock into pieces about the size of a man's fist, which are then ground to a powder.

Separation of the minerals

Next comes separation—a job done until recently by hand. Today man relies on the different properties of minerals—such as weight and colour—to separate the valuable material from the waste.

Liquid sorting and tabling

Some minerals, for instance, are heavy, whilst others are light. When crushed ore is placed in a tank of liquid, some sinks while other parts of it float. So the two are easily collected.

Minerals can also be separated by water and vibration. When a stream of water is pumped over a vibrating table, the minerals are jostled up and down. The light ones are washed away faster than the heavy ones. Such a method of separation is known as *tabling*.

Chemical sorting

Certain minerals are attracted and others rejected by some chemicals. When these chemicals are made into bubbles—rather like the bubbles in a washing-up liquid—the attracted minerals stick to the bubbles. This very important method of mineral separation is called *flotation*.

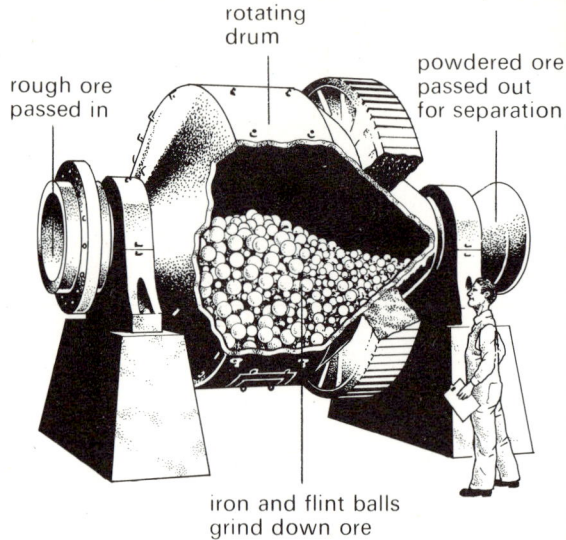

rotating drum

rough ore passed in

powdered ore passed out for separation

iron and flint balls grind down ore

Ore is placed in a rotating mill to be ground down by iron and flint balls. Finer material works its way to one end. Valuable minerals must then be extracted from this powdered ore.

Tabling at a Cornish tin mine: water flows over a vibrating table which can jostle particles of crushed ore. The lighter ones are washed away first. Valuable minerals can be separated in this way.

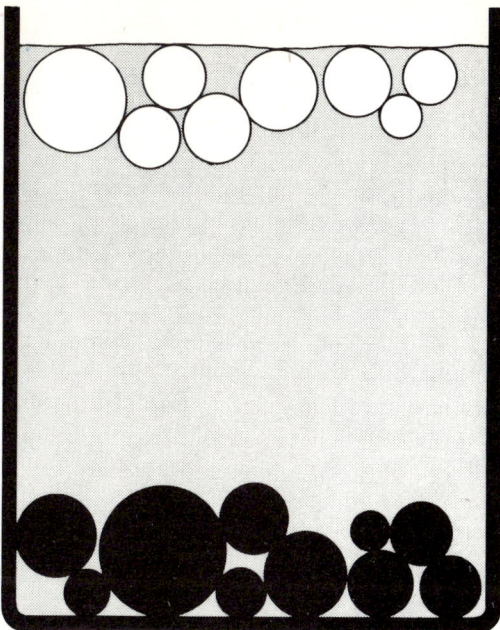

Separating ore in liquid: heavy particles (shown as black spheres) sink, whilst lighter particles (white) float on the surface. The valuable part of the rock can then be removed.

Flotation: certain minerals from the crushed ore are attracted to certain chemicals. The minerals stick to bubbles of these chemicals and in this form they can be floated off and used.

Magnets and static electricity

A few metals like iron are attracted to a magnet. This magnetism is often used to remove them from a mixture of magnetic and non-magnetic materials. Very high powered magnets can now attract material that is only slightly magnetic.

In a similar way that a balloon when rubbed on cloth will stick to the ceiling, some minerals can also be attracted by *electro-static* forces.

Colour sorting

A number of even newer methods are being used more and more often in the mineral processing industry. One is colour sorting. This uses a machine which is sensitive to light or colour.

When, for example, a white mineral passes the electronic eye, it sets off a switch which blows a jet of compressed air out to push the white mineral away from the other colours.

Better use of resources

Mineral processing is often the key to success as far as mining is concerned. Today advances in processing have made it worthwhile to take out rock containing very little valuable material. In doing this we are making much better use of our mineral resources.

We can now sift through the mining dumps left by past generations and make use of what they threw away. In Western Australia gold mining dumps have been re-used, and in Thailand dumps of fluorspar have been reprocessed. Why waste valuable material, after all, when so much time, trouble and money have been spent in removing it from the ground in the first place? As minerals are used up we must ensure that we do not waste Earth's remaining resources.

35

Living with mining

Mines today are bigger than ever before. The Sierrita opencast copper mine in Arizona, USA, mines a massive 92,000 tonnes of ore a day. To obtain this it must create 164,000 tonnes of waste every day. The pit itself covers an area the size of the City of London and is 250 metres deep. The effect that this large-scale mining has on the environment is enormous.

Mining problems

A number of questions are raised by mining activity. Are resources being used up too fast? Are we spoiling the landscape with opencast mines and slag heaps?

Is underground mining causing a danger of subsidence as earth falls in on old workings? Is the industry causing pollution of the air or of water in its processing of minerals? Do the noise and dust and heavy traffic of a mine create problems in populated areas?

Controlling pollution

Because of the scale of modern mining, companies and governments all over the world are looking at the problems in detail. Many governments are now more concerned with pollution of the environment and often have sets of strict laws and regulations. Permission to mine or to make an existing mine larger, particularly in populated areas, is usually strictly controlled.

Practical improvements

In the planning and running of a mine, much can be done to reduce the worst effects. Noise and dust can be reduced by careful scheduling of blasting, cancellation of night working and by washing down trucks before they leave the site. Trees, plants and clever landscaping can conceal slag heaps and tips.

Reclamation

The main problem occurs when the workings are finished with. Mined out landscapes of the last century are a warning to us. Today we care more about *reclamation*. Land reclaimed from mining can eventually be returned to agricultural use, so that few signs of mining remain. Empty pits from mining and quarrying can become attractive lakes for recreation or havens for water birds.

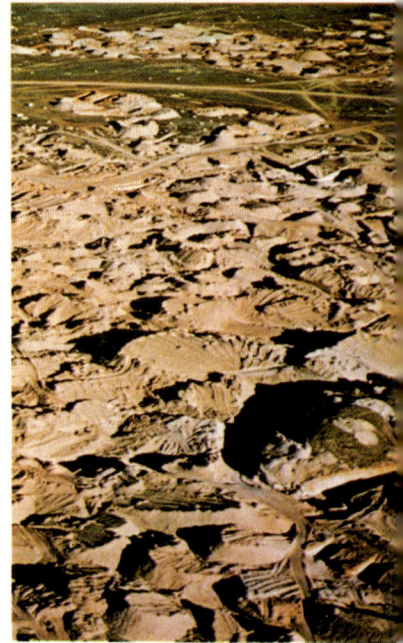

Above: opal mining has badly scarred this Australian landscape.

Below: this gravel pit has been flooded and can now be used for recreation.

Reclamation of land near Dunbar, Scotland. When each strip has been quarried (**above**) it is filled in. It can then be used again as farming land (**below**).

Trade and power

Some countries are rich in mineral resources and others are not. The latter must trade for their mineral needs, as must large producers who use all their own supplies and need more.

Today as ever, minerals, metals and mining knowledge are the key to wealth and power. Because of this, wars, invasion and slavery have often been caused by peoples eager for resources.

Mining wealth

The wealth of large countries such as Australia, Canada and the USA is helped by the richness of their mineral resources. But as science helps us find more and more of the world's deposits, remote and unlikely places suddenly become important.

The barren, uninhabited island of Rockall, off the coast of Britain, is an example. For whichever country rules it owns the rights of the underwater minerals and oil that might be nearby.

New mines

A great copper mine was opened recently on the tiny island of Bougainville in the Pacific Ocean. The islanders had always lived off farming and hunting. Suddenly a town and port had been built on their island, with roads, petrol stations, a landing strip for aircraft and even

OIL (1976)

million tonnes per year

USSR	USA	Saudi Arabia	Iran	Nigeria	UK
518	463	426	295	103	12

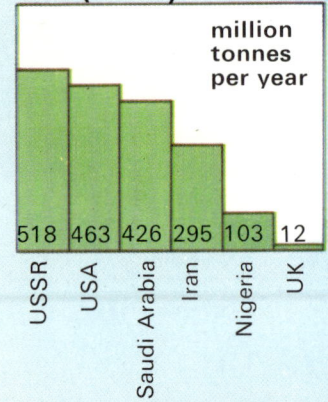

Below: mining diamonds in Borneo.

COAL (1976)

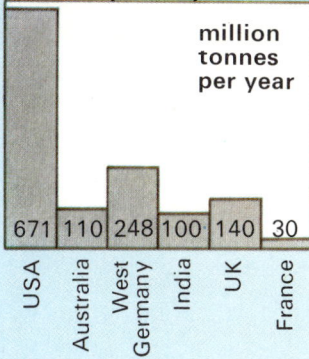

million
tonnes
per year

USA	Australia	West Germany	India	UK	France
671	110	248	100	140	30

IRON ORE (1975)

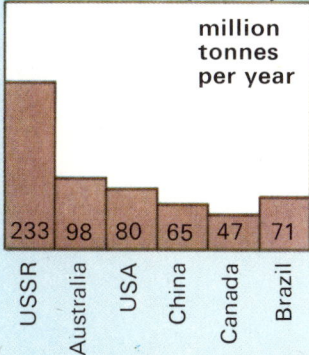

million
tonnes
per year

USSR	Australia	USA	China	Canada	Brazil
233	98	80	65	47	71

Below: a meeting of the members of OPEC.

supermarkets and car parks.

As the example of Bougainville shows, discovery of mineral wealth can change a country overnight. For the newly independent countries of Africa, mining and technology change traditional ways of life, at the same time as they enable the country to trade and become powerful.

Nationalization

Within countries the mining industry is often 'nationalized' or taken over by the State, instead of being run by private companies. Coal mining was nationalized in Britain in 1946.

Treaties and organizations

Mineral resources often form the basis of international agreement. In Europe, the European Coal and Steel Community (1952) was the first step towards the present Economic Community (the EEC).

When a few producers supply the needs of the world, the power of minerals is very great. A few years ago OPEC (the Organization of Petroleum Exporting Countries) increased prices and cut down production. Since they produce about 60% of the world's oil, the effects of their action were felt around the world.

Not only oil producers band together; other organizations include bauxite, copper, iron, tin, lead and mercury producers. These organizations of mineral producers have great power to influence everyday life all over the world.

Minerals of the world

This map shows how minerals are distributed around the world.

Canada has a 3,000 km long gold belt, whilst large copper mines stretch from the Rocky Mountains in western North America to the Andes in South America, itself rich in silver. Africa has many great belts of natural resources—from the copper belt centred in Zambia to the gold, diamond and platinum areas in South Africa. Australia has nickel and gold in the west and lead/zinc in the east. Europe is rich in coal and minerals.

Arctic Ocean

EUROPE

NORTH AMERICA

Atlantic Ocean

AFRICA

Pacific Ocean

SOUTH AMERICA

KEY

○	Oil		Lead and zinc
●	Coal	s	Salt
■	Iron ore	●	Sulphur
■	Uranium	●	Potash
■	Copper	●	Phosphate
◆	Diamonds	◎	Asbestos
◆	Gold and silver	○	Tin

As you look at this map you will notice that minerals are concentrated in certain areas. Often the patterns follow mountains chains: they show the geological history of the continents.

Arctic Ocean

ASIA

Pacific Ocean

Indian Ocean

AUSTRALIA

Mining in the future

Are we running out of our vital raw materials? We cannot really say how the future of mining will turn out. It is certainly true that minerals and fuels are being used up at an alarming rate.

Petroleum consumption, for example, between 1960 and 1970, was the same as that between 1860 and 1960. Because the world's mineral resources are distributed unevenly, some countries have become so used to mineral wealth that they take it for granted and waste it.

Fortunately, people who have wasted minerals in the past are becoming increasingly conscious of saving energy and resources.

The fact that we are using up our resources faster and faster is worrying, but the world is still a vast store of fuel and minerals. In many cases known reserves are higher today than they were twenty years ago.

New inventions

Necessity is the mother of invention. Mining methods have become more efficient. Satellites can now reveal new reserves at greater depths.

Some new inventions are quite incredible. *Bacterial leaching* is one new method of mining. A bomb is used

WORLD OIL PRODUCTION

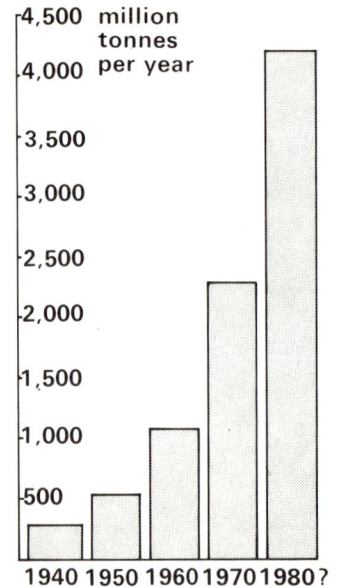

Above: the use of oil has grown alarmingly. It is now possible that it could double every 10-20 years.

Below: A car is scrapped, but the metal can be re-cycled.

to shatter an underground copper or uranium deposit. Bacteria are then pumped down to do the rest. They eat the copper or uranium and are then pumped back to the surface, bringing the mineral with them.

New processing methods can also do wonders, squeezing the last drops out of valuable material. Many materials we use can be replaced by others—plastics can replace glass, wood, lead and even steel.

Recycling

Copper is mined in Chile. The same copper may be smelted in the USA, built into a Japanese car and sold in Europe. But that copper need not be wasted, for the metal can then be re-used when the car is scrapped. The copper does not disappear. It can merely be borrowed for a time. This process of re-use is called *re-cycling*.

New horizons

Unknown new regions may also offer unimagined riches. Russian projects suggest that the frozen Arctic and Antarctic may have rich mineral resources.

The sea itself—70% of the Earth's surface—is a vast and untouched storehouse of minerals and energy. The ocean floor, sea water and even the tides themselves can produce everything from salt and gold to energy.

Looking up from the sea to the sky, who knows what new deposits are to be found in space?

Above: an astronaut collects samples of moon rock.

Below: the *Glomar Challenger* can drill in 6,000 metres of water to probe the Earth's crust.

Books to read

Mining coal, Davey;
A & C Black 1976
Restless Earth, Calder;
BBC 1972
**What do you know
about the Earth?**
Curtis; Hamlyn 1976
The story of the Earth;
HMSO 1973
Volcanoes; HMSO 1974
Discovering the Earth,
Clare; Macdonald
Educational 1974
Inside the Earth, Davis;
Macdonald Educational
1970
The gold diggers,
Driscoll and Hollyer;
Macdonald Educational
1977
The last resource,
Loftus; Pelican 1972
Mineral resources,
Warren; Pelican 1973
**The world's finest
minerals and crystals**
Bancroft; Thames and
Hudson 1973
**The observer's book of
geology,** Evans; Warne
1968

Things to do

Geology is a rewarding
hobby that is easy to
carry out. Rocks and
minerals can be easily
collected in the
countryside, particularly
in mining areas. Take
care. Mines and old
mining areas can be
dangerous places to
wander around alone.
However, many
companies do take parties
of interested people and
show them how it is done
—school parties are
particularly welcome. The
natural geology of Britain
can best be seen in the
National Parks—the Peak
District is famous for
limestone country and
Snowdonia and the Lake
District for volcanic rocks
and slate. Happy
hunting . . .

Places to go

Many museums have a
collection of rocks and
minerals, all named with
details of origin, location,
age, elements contained
etc. Some specimens can
be truly spectacular and
so rare that you will
probably only see them in
the glass case.
Nevertheless, you should
try and find your own
specimens and start a
private collection.

In Kensington, London,
the Geological Museum
has a splendid collection
of rocks, minerals and
gems. Several exhibitions
illustrate geological
topics. Around the corner
is the Natural History
Section of the British
Museum; rocks and
minerals are joined by a
vast collection of fossils
ranging from minute
microfossils to the giant
dinosaurs.

Outside London most
museums in the major
cities have a mineral
collection. Liverpool has
the City Museum,
Manchester the University
Museum, Newcastle-
upon-Tyne the Hancock
Museum, and Nottingham
its own Natural History
Museum. In the
south-west, Plymouth has
a collection of local rocks
and the Camborne School
of Mines has an
exhibition open to the
public. The National
Museums of Scotland and
Wales have large rock and
fossils collections in
Edinburgh and Cardiff.
Scotland also has the
Royal Burgh Museum of
Dumfries.

Glossary

Here is a list of some of the more difficult terms used in mining.

Abrasive: A hard resistant material used to rub surfaces smooth.
Adit: A tunnel dug into a hillside to reach minerals that are to be mined.
Alloy: A mixture of a metal and another metal or non-metal.
Bit: The cutting end of the drill.
Blasting: Breaking rock and ore into smaller loose fragments using explosives.
Cage: The lift which transports men, ore, and supplies between the surface and underground.
Crude oil: Natural oil as it is taken from the ground before being refined.
Derrick: A frame used to hold the drilling rods on a rig.
Dragline: A giant crane with a large bucket to scoop up rock.
Dredge: A ship that uses a suction pipe or a bucket chain to scoop up minerals from under water.
Flotation: Separation of the various parts of an ore by chemical bubbles.
Hydraulic mining: Extracting minerals from rock with high-powered water hoses.

Igneous rock: Rock solidified from magma.
Magma: Molten rock found beneath the Earth's surface.
Metamorphic rock: Rock formed from igneous or sedimentary rock by changes in temperature, pressure, and chemical fluids.
Metal: A chemical element or alloy. Often a shiny solid, good at conducting electricity or heat.
Mineral: A general term for the substances that make up rocks.
Opencast mining: The extraction of rock and minerals from a large hole or quarry on the surface.
Ore: A rock as it is mined, containing valuable material that can be extracted.
Orebody: A deposit of rich ore.
Overburden: Material such as soil or rock which lies above a valuable mineral deposit.
Petroleum reservoir: a band of porous rock containing petroleum.
Plate: A section of the Earth's crust.
Porous rock: Rock that can soak up liquid.
Prop: A block of wood or metal used to support the roof of a mine.
Prospector: Somebody who explores for minerals.
Reclamation: The improvement of land

after mining has finished, so that it can be used once again.
Re-cycling: The re-use of metal and minerals.
Refinery: A factory for purifying and processing petroleum and gas.
Rig: A platform, truck, or vessel that carries drilling equipment.
Resources: The wealth of minerals that have not yet been mined.
Seam: a layer of valuable mineral below the ground, usually coal.
Sedimentary rock: Rocks built up by the gathering together of loose grains of rock.
Shaft: A vertical tunnel connecting the underground mine with the surface.
Slag: The solid material that floats to the surface of a molten mass of metal during smelting.
Slurry: A mixture of solid material and water.
Smelt: To melt ore in order to extract and purify the metal.
Solution mining: Extracting minerals from underground by dissolving the mineral in water, and bringing it to the surface.
Underground mining: Extracting minerals from below the ground by a shaft and a series of tunnels.
Vein: A strip of usually valuable mineral cutting through the Earth's crust.

Index

Illustrations appear in bold type.